of Grief & Greatness

Sonnets by
Jessa R. Sexton

HILLIARD
PRESS

Of Grief & Greatness

Written by Jessa R. Sexton
Book Block & Cover Design by Whitnee Clinard
Artwork by Rebecca Mayes

Published by Hilliard Press
a division of The Hilliard Institute

Franklin, Tennessee
Oxford, England

www.hilliardinstitute.com

# of Grief & Greatness

Sonnets by
Jessa R. Sexton

Table of Contents

Dedication

For fellow writers of rhythm and rhyme—let's bring
poetry back.

Special Thanks

I'd like to thank my editors and sonnet consultants—
Amber Bartlett, Mattea Gernentz, Lauren Haynes,
K. Mark Hilliard, Rosemary J. Hilliard, Kate Lala,
Becca Osborn, and Aleta Stewart.

I also must thank Rebecca Mayes (@rebletters)
for creating the roses and handlettering on the
cover as well as the three coloring pages in the
devotionals. Also, thank you, Whitnee Clinard for
always presenting me with the exact book design I'm
dreaming of.

Finally, thank you, Patsy Clairmont, for spending
time helping me brainstorm ways to make this book
more accessible, applicable, and interactive.

A Note

I have at least sixteen journals. You can find them
scattered around my house: beside my bed and
favorite writing chair; inside my piano bench and
every purse or bag I might use; and even in my
hand, depending on if you catch me in a moment of
inspiration. The journals are filled with lines, lyrics,
and scraps of paper with other lines and lyrics.

I'm not one to wax nostalgic about life before
computers as I ignore their productive use. Trust me.
If I'm writing anything lengthy, I'm on my laptop. But
poetry. That tends to start differently for me. I love
the feeling of pencil and paper—the grey, rubbed out
mess of left-behind words as newer and better ones
take their place. Not every poem or song I write meets
its completion on paper, but most start there.

Speaking of starts—in 2004, I wrote my first sonnet.
In 2011, I became obsessed with them. In 2014, I
wrote the first poem that appears in this book. In
2016, I published a book of fairy tales condensed into
sonnets. I've had a long relationship with this form.

The poems in these pages weren't written for publication. They weren't written assuming you'd one day hold this book in your hands. They were the ponderings of my pencil and my heart. But in the summer of 2017, I thought to myself: why not? Why not publish them? I've shared one here and there throughout the years when I thought a topic would help someone through a particular life moment. I know poetry isn't popular. But I believe God's gifted me in this way of writing, and I believe that He will, somehow, use these words for His good.

Several near to my heart have experienced overwhelming grief as I worked on this project; loss and pain are a natural part of the human experience, which is why my poetry is often inspired by the confusion and darkness of this time. I send my love to these loved ones.

My hope is not to antagonize any aching souls but to explore the extremes in life, for even in our pain He is present. Today is full of moments of grief and greatness (and the calm and sometimes mundane in between). But I know that tomorrow is held by the One of Ultimate Greatness. In this knowledge, I find the strength to press on. In this knowledge, I find the joy to celebrate.

These poems are a mirror of my mind. They reflect, in an anxious intimacy, both how broken and how hopeful I am.

These poems are a gift to you. In the back you'll find a topical index. Use it to guide your eyes to words that will (I pray) meet you where you are in the moment.

These poems are a journey for us. I've walked with them thus far, and now I invite you to walk through them with me.

The Sonnets

You may notice a bit more of a "stiffness" to the rhythm of this poem, compared to the others you'll soon read. However, I felt compelled to include it, as it was the first in my series of scriptural sonnets. When I studied Joel several years ago, I was inspired; I realized this same storyline—grief caused by sinning and drifting from God, grace in the darkness, glory in His presence— is as raw and relevant today as it was in the time of this prophet. We need this message: no matter how much of a stranger we've been to Him, He's calling us back. And when we return, He will be our home.

Joel

Somehow you've loved the deepdown soul in me.
Embracing Grace, you hid me from danger,
though I'd been quiet long—a soft stranger.
You still felt fit to grant me fresh pity,
when you saw—in and outward—my mourning;
I, deserving nothingness or anger,
throwing up of hands, "We'll never change her,"
was instead restored, satisfied in thee—
offered a hand to lift me from my shame,
pulled from darkness into luminescence.
And now I hear you calling—not to blame—
to bring holiness, wholiness reclaim
so I can know again of your presence:
the blessing-best, shared with me! Praise His name!

Mark 9:24 is one of my absolute favorite Bible verses. The rawness and realness to these words ring loudly through my heart: "I believe—help thou now my unbelief." *Yes, Lord. I DO believe in you, yet something inside worries or confuses or allures me. Make my faith solid and sure.* In my writing, I find myself returning to this verse. A sonnet is tidy and complex, and here I've made it messy with enjambment and also repetitive, just as "belief...unbelief" repeats the truth of this father's heart as he cries out for his son to be healed by The Son. Furthermore, an Italian sonnet style (used here) itself cries out, "Abba, Abba!" in its rhyme scheme (abba abba cd cd ee). Therefore, it was the perfect form to function my intent.

Father and Son

Help thou now my unbelief: I want to
know I know; cease this peaceless part of me,
this pierced fear that seeks to keep honestly
questioning questions with a cold and true
panic that leads the thieves of fullness through
my then empty demi-heart. Guarantee
Everafter every day; let would-be
telltales fail to filch my faith. Please pursue
me, and—as a hunter takes aim (only,
I welcome your arrows of actual-
ity)—pierce these fierce perplexities: free-
dom comes not when thoughts run free. Rationale
tells me this tells me that tells me tales fails
me. Crush all qualms as regnant ease prevails.

Mark 9:24

As a poet, I often find a tiny phrase resonating in my head. I write them in journals or on bits of paper. Some phrases sit forever on a page; some evolve: the latter occurred with this poem. I visualized God's grace as a physical canopy (both a tree and an umbrella coming to mind) protecting me with its covering. We tend to swing from one side to the other with grace: either we hear nothing about it at all or we are overwhelmed with the topic to the point of ignoring our own responsibility towards righteous living. For me, grace is a concept I combat not because of those extreme teachings, but because of its extreme simplicity—which I make complex through my human reasoning. With this poem, I invite us to think about His presence, protection, and preeminence enveloping our each and every day.

Canopy of Grace

If you choose to lie beneath His cano-
py of grace, resting in hope (the sacred
place of active assurance) that manna
will come to your wilderness; that lucid
meaning will be made of your madness (and,
when it is not, that you can walk the way
supported, solid, strengthened by His hand);
that humility might mean your faults splayed
out, your heart caved in, your eyes full, and your
mouth empty; and that your nothing plus His
everything still equals everything—sure
of your slightness and His capaciousness:
then prepare yourself to be always awed,
and to grapple with the greatness of God.

In a moment of intense self-doubt, I asked God why He was leading me a certain direction. I rationalized with Him about my weaknesses. He knew everything I was telling Him, and He knew I was trying to get away from the calling He was placing on me. "You say you can't do it; you're right. Make way for a movement of faith." I've heard over and over again in my life that God will equip you for the task He calls you to. However, sometimes that isn't the complete story. Right now, God is telling me that *He is my equipment.* I can't. He can. And He's here. That's what is important. That's how I will make it through—that's how I will depart from the slavery of my self-doubt. My exodus.

My Exodus

So now, go. I don't care what you think your
weaknesses are; I am your strength. You say
you can't do it; you're right: I can. Make way
for a movement of faith. I don't send for
perfect people—because there are none. Nor
do I call only the confident: pray
your confidence comes from me—every day.
Quiet the counterfeiter I deplore.
He says you're inept for my intent—as
if that matters. Because the Promised Land
isn't reached by your mere achievements. No.
I'm here with you: if I give you a path
and a purpose, I'll give you a map and
a means. You said, "Here am I," so now, go!

Exodus 3   *Isaiah 6:8*

The New Testament Letters are a source of constant inspiration to me. This particular sonnet was written in a Bible class on Ephesians Chapter One (hence the precise yet non-poetic title). The power that raised Christ from the dead is alive in us! Because of His grace and love, we are to be His light of love to others. As you read this poem, I hope the use of second person pronouns draws "you" in, as if Paul is speaking not to those of Ephesus long ago, but to us directly today.

Ephesians 1

Ever thankful am I for you—and ev-
er thanks I give for you. I pray for great
wisdom; as you grow in your knowledge, nev-
er let your hearts grow dim—rather, create
vast floods of light that will shine radiant
confidence of the hope in our inher-
itance. I pray you know, with evident
awe, that the same greatness—beyond compare—
that raised Christ from the dead and placed beneath
Him all other authority—that same
power lives in and for those who believe.
All praise to God who, through Christ, made us blame-
less. (How can that be!?) Before He made the
world—He loved us! And His grace makes us free!

When I read Hebrews 11, I imagine these names etched on a memorial wall, my fingers tracing the outline of each letter. If we had lived then, would we be listed here? As we live now, do we manifest the mannerisms of these faithful followers? This poem was written as I considered my own convictions. I admit I'm not where I want to be, but much of our journey as Christians is in acceptance of our current state and refusal to stay there. Onward we rise.

Hebrews 11

Can my faith become the confidence those
of the past were commended for? Command-
ed to existence, my universe, cho-
sen by Him to follow Him, must remand—
must reprimand any part of me that
seeks self service over sacrifice to
that unseen cause of holy fear. While at
the offering table, do I renew
His pleasure in me? I connect with feel-
ing as the alien in a strange land—
but am I willing to wait for the real
reward when what I see's not what I planned?

I want kingdom-conquering, bond-embrac-
ing, full wall-crumbling, death-dashing faith.

"Less is More" begins with a juxtaposition of greater and lesser. The first lines speak not of God actually becoming any greater (as His greatness is supreme), but of my **acceptance** and **acknowledgement** of this fact. When we embrace this truth, our lives will alter. We will be humbled. However, if we think humility is unattractive, we misunderstand humility. Our lessening of self doesn't mean we abandon the qualities that make us "fearfully and wonderfully made," but that we relinquish our unrighteousness in exchange for His restoration. This isn't a fair trade: we end up with so much more. We gain forever.

Less is More

He must become greater, as I become
less, for He's greater, far greater indeed,
than anything I am or think I need.
This I know, and in this I am undone,
because all this talk has not yet begun
its work in me until I truly lead
a life guided by the fact He'll exceed,
really exceed, all my other wants. From
there, and there only, can I move forward;
then my humility shall be honored
as I draw near and am drawn near to Him.

From desolation, I can be restored.
Through generous grace, my sin is conquered.
Less of myself brings more of Christ within.

James 4: 5-10   John 3:30   1 Peter 5:4-10

Esther 4:14 will forever connect in my heart to the stories of Joseph, of Moses, of Paul, and of Jessa. No, I don't claim to hold the honor these others deserve, but I have felt the same confirming conviction: no matter—and because of—what I've done and where I've been—I am here. Now. Right where I'm supposed to be *for such a time as this*. Big and small, momentous and mundane: *for such a time as this*. I may never save a nation, but I pray I take part in saving a soul. Esther braved a king. Moses a pharaoh. Paul the God-fearing and godless alike. Joseph those who had betrayed him. Because His grace covers us, we can pay grace forward. We're here to hear Him—to hear how we can serve Him here. We may not understand how today, but the moment we are in is for Him.

Joseph

For such a time as this, I am here. No
harm intended will conquer the greatness
God can grant in this moment. And although
hate favors hate, love can overcome. Blessed
beyond and even through my past, I can
accept my present presence. I am here—
wholly where I am supposed to be, stand-
ing unholy before the Holy, clear-
ly quieted, warily aware of
my own flailing failings as I fathom
that forgiving others in His lush love—
no matter the depth of their deeds—becomes
an opportunity to take part in
the miracle of Grace defeating sin.

"What is the meaning of life?" I've known the answer to this ultimate question for many years: the meaning of life is to love and be loved. Colossians 3 explains clearly that we are nothing without love. God is love (1 John 4:8). God loved us enough to sacrifice His son that we may live (John 3:16). Though this is a gift we cannot warrant, repay, or reciprocate—knowledge of our salvation must cause us to change. We walk His way peacefully and gratefully, satisfied and serving: we accept His love and, in turn, love others. This is our purpose. This brings Him praise.

Love and Be Loved

Over all your virtues—compassion, kind-
ness, humility, gentleness, and pa-
tience—put on love, for all efforts unbind,
unwind, grow unrefined...cause falls away
without love. Called to love, called to peace: you
must live with a grateful heart—be content.
You carry the Best News; in all you do—
as you speak, act, and live—you represent
Him. Do everything in His name, in His
honor, as you give thanks to God—and here
lies the key to contentment: no task is
meaningless when we mean to praise. If we're
striving for fulfillment, we've lost our way
unless we're serving in Him every day.

Colossians 3

We spend too much of our time losing at the comparison game. But guess what: someone else being strong doesn't make us weak. God didn't create us to be good at everything, no matter how desperately we want the world to assume such. This humble truth about our being proportional rather than perfect should be a weight lifted instead of a burden borne. Rather than being consumed by an endless amount of functions, we can focus on turning our true talents into ways to praise His name, aid those in need, and raise our self-confidence. When we align our lives in such a way to bring Him glory through our gifts, we find a fulfillment for both today and Tomorrow.

Called

Be honest with yourself, humble in Him,
and helpful with your gift—whether that gift
is communicating, serving those when
those (maybe) don't even know, teaching, lift-
ing the fallen through encouragement, giv-
ing graciously and generously, lead-
ing with respect, or being kind. We live
our gifts in gratefulness, knowing we need
the Gifter. See, hear, move, aid, lead, heal, or
interpret. What makes your heart sing, your eyes
fill with tears—what stirs your searching soul? For
this movement of your very being ties
you to your community calling—see
dreams turn you to the one you're meant to be.

Romans 12:3—9   1 Corinthians 12

Inside each sonnet are pieces of my heart. After my thoughts have condensed themselves into their new, tidy pentameter, I read them out aloud. This is my poetry process, to pause my writing throughout, reading portions out loud over and over and over. Sometimes the words on my lips possess an intensity—a thrill from verbalizing so perfectly what I was feeling. When I write with the first person perspective from God to myself as I have done in this poem, I can hear His rebukes and reassurances in my own voice. In "Their Bright Arrivals," God tells us to make preparations for a closeness with Him. We must admit the things that tempt us, acknowledge that nothing other than Him will truly fill us, and accept our human limitations— perfection is not even a possibility. However, we can conquer all of these things because we know He is on the other side of our humility, ready with an honor and ardor that shines beyond any momentary ray of today.

Their Bright Arrivals

Build up! Build up! Prepare the road! Clear out
the rocks and stones that keep you from my side.
Let go of your expectations about
somehow earning my love—like dignified
deeds can save you when your heart is captive
to—captivated by—sundry idols
and ideals. Can these feckless attractive
ambitions save you? Their bright arrivals
grow dim in the light of their glaring re-
treats. And who will fill you when they run dry?
Why do you try so hard to possess the
possibility of perfection? I,
the one absolute, shall restore, renew;
when you fall low, I'll raise and adore you.

Isaiah 57: 12—15

In 1826, University of Oxford graduate and award-winning poet Reginald Heber wrote the lyrics to one of my favorite hymns. "Holy, holy, holy! Lord God Almighty! Early in the morning, our song shall rise to thee." "Live in the Wonder of God" is inspired by Heber's hymn, Isaiah 6:3, and Psalm 8:3-4 (which I explore even more singularly in the sonnet "And All Those Stars"). Throughout the poem on the adjacent page, I pose a series of questions, all with the same main idea: how on earth can we so easily ignore the wonders of our Lord? Flip to the back of the book for Heber's hymn lyrics and a full devotional on this poem.

Live in the Wonder of God

"Holy, holy, holy is the Lord Al-
mighty: all earth is full of His glory."
Call me then into your presence—enthrall
me with the awesomeness of your story.

Why does dullness pervade my days? Surround-
ed by the evercasting light of the
Everlasting Might of my God—dumbfound-
ed awe should prevail: not complacency.

But blindness to beauty becomes simple.
Too simple. Why? When the Maker of those
marvelous stars (all those stars!), is mindful
of me—in my frozen phase, I'm still chos-
en—why can't I live in the wonder of
God, when all earth is a sign of His love?

Isaiah 6:3

One day I plan to write sonnets on all of the major religious holidays, but at this point "Easter" is my first and only. I kept thinking about the contrasts Easter poses. The empty tomb was the fullness of His attained promise. Death was an end to His physical self, yet the resurrection was the true beginning of our spiritual selves. And when we accept how lost we are, we reach a starting point to finding Him. Many don't understand or value the consequence of the cross, the weightiness of the rock that was rolled away, the import of His ascension. But those of us who know Him know, and we will never be the same.

Easter

Never have we been more full than when He
fulfilled all that was and is and is to
come with emptiness. And never have few-
er final breaths hard held the weight of the
sins of the entire world. Our would-be
deaths died, yet some quietly misconstrue
and demean the scene of the cross, world view-
ing that beginning as an end when three
days brought another beginning within.
Never have we felt so foundedly lost
than when we knew we needed to be found.
Why do we worry if He sees our skin,
like that first time in the Garden? The cost
was canceled. We're on Resurrection Ground.

My poetry is sometimes a tight commingling of scripture and personal experience. "Exodus 9" is one such poem. As I listened to a familiar Bible story, Pharaoh's hard heart despite God's continually obvious opulence, I thought about certain people in my life who have brought destruction to others because they were unable to see past their narrow fascinations and aspirations. I pray the vulnerability I have allowed myself to share here is meaningful for you. Hard hearts are ignorant of others, and become ignorant even of self. If we allow ourselves to become so fixed on obtaining a goal no matter the cost, we will waste energies that could be used for His glory.

Exodus 9

Tomorrow He will work wonders under
your open eyes, but your hard heart won't see,
can't agree, there just might be another
side. Instead you heap debris on debris,
add injury to injury: a care-
less, helpless heaped mess of brokenness left
bereft in the wake of your unaware
annihilation. Pain made manifest
in your resistance, in all that distance
you pile up between us, between your wants
and His way. Just harness that persistence,
instead, toward acknowledging the response
always appropriate in any case—
a humble acceptance of His grand grace.

What writer isn't fascinated by wordplay? *Altar* and *alter*: these two homophones were made for each other. As I considered the altar of the past, a physical place to offer death as a humble request for life, and the altar of today, a spiritual place to offer one's life in thankfulness for His death, the next poem began to take shape. Our time in prayer, in devotion to Him, should change us. We shouldn't be afraid to give up the small things of our mortality for the vast offering of His immortality. And the ultimate truth—that His greatness isn't dependent upon our acceptance or praise of Him—is hopefully a kind of freedom to love Him not because He needs us, but because He loves us as well.

Altar of Alteration

Meet and speak with me at the altar of
my prayer—so I can set down everything
and humbly alter there. For there's no love
that's stronger than the one in your being,
and I'm ready to sacrifice my blind-
ness for your seeing. I hold hope that no
one—no thing—can separate; you will find
me, bind me, kindly, profoundly—no glow
of any star can outshine the God you
are! You don't need my offering to sit
up on your throne and reign. You don't need new
temples built, or old ones built again. It
dawns on me that your need for me is sole:
that I love, live, and build unholy whole.

All of my poems are personal, but some are intensely so, such as "Romans 12:21." I can remember reading this oft-quoted scripture and thinking "easier said than done," which I hope I've put in far more poetic terms in this sonnet. Though I intend to meet difficult people or situations with grace and goodness, "when my intentions meet my completions," do they equal out? Not often enough. Because loving someone who doesn't show us love is next to impossible given our human nature. Sometimes I grow tired of being the bigger person because it's far simpler to be the bitter person. But in the end, we want to be on the side of goodness— the winning side!—so we cannot expect to switch teams at the last minute. This means we're forced to give up some of our controlling nature, but the reward of true freedom stands on the other side of that sacrifice. Eternity is of more value than ego. If we can see past today, we can overcome whatever today brings us.

Romans 12:21

"Do not be overcome by evil, but
overcome evil with good." I repeat
these neat words—but they aren't so tidy put
into practice. When my intentions meet
my completions, where's the equality?
How can I reach for that which I'll never
reach? Or love one who will never love me?
I'm overwhelmed by the task of sever-
ing my ego from my actions—I need
strength to be weak—to be vulnerable—
because I can't do this alone! What free-
dom is worth the bondage of lost control?

Yours. So each day—no matter peers or pride—
I'll side with good—for Goodness shall abide.

Sometimes I grow livid at the voice of lies in my heart that keeps me from living purposefully. *All we have is now. You deserve better. You've made too many mistakes to be effective for Him.* These seemingly contradictory lines do their best work when God is presenting me with a task I make impossible by my own obsessions. This sonnet carries more bleakness with it because its intent is to remind us how easily we become incapacitated for His purpose by our own doing. Temptation's best work in us is often to create individuals so self-absorbed by desire or doubt that we have no time for Him. We can neither love nor be loved until we are ready to cast off these concerns and move forward in His mercy.

Incapacitated

Get behind me, temptation, your concern
is here, now—you are immediate, not
eternal; fixed, not forever; unearned,
not invested; and self-seeking, not sought.
You know my every weakness, impress up-
on my common sense, and take advantage
of my ignorance until nothing of
my world makes sense but you. Or else you dredge
up my past—presenting how bleak my fu-
ture stands—stained severely—restraining an-
y chance at change in self or others. True—
you know what to say so that I'll stay stand-
ing static while my self obsession melts
all chance of sharing love with someone else.

Symbolism is one of the richest elements of a story. In Nehemiah 5:13, the minor prophet shakes his robes as a representation of the warning he shares: "In the same way I shake out my garments, may God shake out those who do not keep their promise to follow Him." Visually, we can see Nehemiah acting this out; this image made me think about requesting that God empty out the sins in our hearts—specifically those of living a false life, giving in to discontent, and misusing our gifts. My repetition of the line "sent for His service...set apart for His service" is intentional and for emphasis. Galatians 5:13 explains that the freedom we find in Him shouldn't be used to follow desires that lead us away from Him. Once again my poetry reflects on life's purpose: acknowledgement of His greatness and grace means living a life of love as we faithfully serve Him and others.

Nehemiah

As I shake out the fold of my garment,
so may God shake and empty out my heart.
A simple sin—to become what we aren't—
we can avoid if we accept content-
ment over entitlement. We are sent
for His service, rebuilding and impart-
ing—living with the truth: we're set apart
for His service; walking always in bent
humility—in the fear of the Lord—
is of more value than any earth-gain.
Never the same, I am changed by His grace,
transformed by the One who will guide me toward
acceptance that my frailty will remain
while His supremacy is to be praised.

Nehemiah 5

You won't likely find me in a chapel, worship, or Bible study setting without a journal and pen. If you do, you'll soon catch me scribbling on whatever I can find with whatever I can find. Inspiration hits me as I hear others talk about God, and my current way to process my spiritual feelings and discoveries is through sonnet writing. Something about the counting of syllables and setting up of rhyme structures creates the perfect avenue for me to explore a verse or concept. The words of the next poem came pouring out of my pencil in chapel one Monday afternoon. Lines three through eight were heavy on my heart as I worshipped that hour. The "transition moments" in life can be the hardest. God doesn't always reveal where we're going or why we've just suffered or even how our present situations have meaning, but we still have to "accept this duration" and keep moving forward with Him. Maybe the lesson is to stop asking so many questions, which is hard for this "control fiend in remission." But there is no one better to trust in all times than the One who was and is and is to come.

My Hope's Foundation

My Hope's foundation—movement without in-
timidation—this, a proclamation
of your solid truth, will give me peace when
no clear path points to your restoration.
Though in supplication I plead to know—
you grant yet no revelation except
that I should accept this duration, go-
ing forward though realization is kept
covered. In every situation, with
prayer and petition, I bring this condi-
tion of concern to you, asking for swift
soothing of a heart heavy in transi-
tion. This control fiend in remission's guid-
ed with a faith built on the crucified.

He is here: here I humbly offer, once again, the only consolation I have in times of ultimate despair. Two of my favorite people lost their babies, and a couple I've loved for years lost their grandson—all in the span of two weeks. I had nothing to offer them, other than peeling back the layers of new skin from my own soul wounds long enough to stand in their sorrow as I wrote this poem. Reliving a lowness only He helped me rise above brought these words. How can a broken heart mend when the pieces are so fragmented that they appear impossible to reassemble? We will suffer, and scriptures confirm that we will become stronger (1 Peter 5:10) and be delivered (Psalm 34:19), but in the moment of misery that future can seem impossibly far away. *Lord, we know things will be good again—but we don't know when. In this time, may your presence offer peace. And please, make this time pass quickly, so that we may soon be on the other side, offering a hand of solace to someone else in sorrow as we repeat what got us through: He is here.*

His Presence

I know you have said that my suffering
is temporal, ephemeral, but this
moment full of anguish I can't dismiss:
I'm lost in it. Utterly. Everything
they say is in kindness, but not bringing
me comfort. My shattered, slivered heart sits,
fragmented, how can it mend when the bits
have forgotten how they fit? Lingering
in this emptiness is useless—I know—
but I didn't ask to bear this partic-
ular cross. Deep-seated sorrow's only
solace is Your presence. Lay waste my woe;
cover me completely. Lord, restore quick-
ly this wreck. Make me whole. Make me holy.

2 Corinthians 4:16-18

Balaam: most of us associate him as the guy in the Old Testament who hit his donkey. I remembered that and only that from this Bible story as I reread it in a Wednesday night study on the book of Numbers. That evening, I learned not only how much of the story I'd missed in my childhood, but also how closely it links to our lives today. In the back of this book, I have a complete devotional on this particular sonnet, but here I want to open by introducing the main theme I ruminated on: God is calling us to live with obedient hearts. Are we ready to listen and follow His lead?

Balaam

I see you standing in the way against
me, in truth for my own benefit—so
I may speak only of and from you. Since
the intent of my actions, I now know,
dictates whether or not I'm honoring
your orders with an obedient heart,
why do I still feel like maneuvering,
manipulating, modifying part
of your plan to better suit my schemes, to
alter your aims for my gains? How many
times does it take—even after I view
unmistakable signs of your plenty-
proof—for me to move forward in firm faith,
fulfilling your functions in me each day?

Numbers 22-24

Psalm 8:3-4 is one of my favorite passages. The slight mention I grant it in "Live in the Wonder of God" doesn't do justice to words that mean so much to my heart. They deserved their own sonnet. I wanted to build up God's magnificence before posing what many of us sometimes find hard to believe: the Creator of *all those stars* made, knows, and loves each and every one of us. Even when we are able to accept the obviousness of His dominion, we sometimes lag in our acknowledgement of His devotion. Any time you feel lacking in love, read this reassurance.

And All Those Stars

When I look up into your Heavens, just
another obviousness of your pure
illustriousness—with eyes wide—I must
admire immensely the work of your
hands: the moon, the stars, every single one
hung in its space place. Your majestic name's
proclaimed throughout your domain—I'm undone
by your glaring glory as the night claims
your replete reign. And still—you know me. As
tiny as I am in the grand scheme of
the skies—still you know me: my flaws, dreams, paths.
What am I that you're mindful of me? Love
me through and because of who I am, who
you are. I'll never know. But I thank you.

Psalm 8:3-4

Have you ever been forced to leave behind the life you were sure you'd been intended to live? I have. And in those moments, my prayers were wracked with questioning. *Why did you bring me here if here is not where I'm supposed to stay?* Analysis of these words shows their foolishness, of course—most lives are not static. However, when the past was beautiful and is ripped from us in an ugly manner—how are we to comprehend this? How can we move on when we don't want to? I return in this sonnet to my frequented theme of God's constant presence being our main source of reassurance in times of transition, turmoil, or treachery. Here, though, Isaiah 43:18-19 brings us an added layer of comfort in the chaos. Not only is God near in our wilderness, He's bringing us out of it and into a lushness we cannot imagine. If we will forget the past and follow in faith, He will lead us on to better.

On To Better

"Forget what once was; don't dwell on the past.
Why? I'm doing something new—something e-
ven better. You'll grow, bloom, thrive—unsurpassed!
I'll make a way through the wasteland. Just be-
lieve." I pray you find ease in these words, in
the knowledge that restoration is com-
ing. I know it doesn't seem so now, when
the pain of this moment has made you numb-
ly bitter, wordless, and alternating
between being completely devoid of
tears to drowning in their devastating
flow. But please remember—He's here, in love,
guiding you away from this wilderness
of woe and into His vast faithfulness.

Isaiah 43:18-19

Turning an entire Psalm into a sonnet was a joyful challenge for me. When my former student (who did the hand lettering and rose drawing for the cover of this book) told me this was one of her favorite passages, I wanted to see if it communicated to me as well, and I couldn't believe how closely it aligned to moments in my life and how quickly the words of this poem came to me. Overwhelmed by opposition—people, responsibilities, burdens—we can become isolated by seemingly insurmountable moments in life. How many times have I prayed "I cannot do it alone!" only to hear "You aren't alone!" Psalm 3 soothes and strengthens our spirits. No enemy—even the one who claims our faith is foolish—can overcome Him, and He is on our side. We don't cry out to nothingness; we are heard by the Everything.

Psalm 3

In this moment, I am thoroughly wear-
y of my adversaries. I've lost count—
I feel so surrounded, confounded, fear-
fully bound in by tasks I can't surmount
on my own. But I'm not alone! At my
lowest—feeling unnoticed—this remiss
poet knows all those around me deny
that You will provide. Yet in faith I dis-
miss their words as absurd. For I know though
I have drifted from you, I'm now lifted
by you. My heart has been heard. My sorrow,
once sated, has been abated. Rifted
no longer from Your presence, I—once shamed,
now reclaimed—am ever-blessed by Your name.

For some reason, I decided that I needed twenty-five sonnets for this book. But when that number landed in my head, I had created only twenty. I've placed them here in the order (best as I remember considering some were in pieces of journals here and there) they were written. "Broken, Never Defeated" was the final, and when I sent it to my parents for their feedback, only moments after tweaking the final couplet, I was astonished at their warm praise. I felt the poem was adequate, but not exceptional. It was so easy to write and simple in nature, but I think those very qualities were key to my parents' connection. Do you ever feel like a Bible verse was written directly to you? My family has endured much the past several years, and Galatians 6:7-16 sings hope. "Today's pains are circumvented by His surpassing grace, unrelenting love, and fast faithfulness." This sonnet is dedicated to my parents, who show me time and again what real strength, integrity, and faith look like. Because of their example, I know that though I may be broken, I am never defeated. We have all felt the intensities presented by this sonnet. I pray that you, too, find reassurance in my rhyme.

Broken, Never Defeated

The world may curse me, but it cannot crush
me, for even in my bewilderment,
I am content, confident because much
more awaits. Today's pains are circumvent-
ed by His surpassing grace, unrelent-
ing love, and fast faithfulness. I am not
abandoned when afflicted or torment-
ed. Though I'll be beaten, broken, and brought
low, I'm never defeated. I'm strong, sought
by a Savior who died so I can live
and breathe and find my meaning in Him. Brought
to His presence, this determinative
moment dashes despair with fortitude.
Though body withers, my soul is renewed.

Galatians 6:7-16

Three Devotionals

Devotional #1
"Joseph"

Start

Esther 4:14 will forever connect in my heart to the stories of Joseph, of Moses, of Paul, and of Jessa. No, I don't claim to hold the honor these others deserve, but I have felt the same confirming conviction: no matter—and because of—what I've done and where I've been—I am here. Now. Right where I'm supposed to be for such a time as this. Big and small, momentous and mundane: for such a time as this. We're here to hear Him—to hear how we can serve Him here. We may not understand how today, but the moment we are in is for Him.

See

Joseph's brothers were so envious of their father's favorite, they threw him into a pit and then sold him into slavery. But God didn't leave him there. As Joseph rose in favor with his master, the man's sinful wife tried to ruin his reputation with lies despite Joseph's steadfast integrity. He was thrown into prison. But God didn't leave him there. Joseph's God-given gift of dream interpretation rewarded him with a high-ranking position under the Pharaoh of Egypt. In this job, with God's wisdom guiding him, Joseph was able to help the Egyptians prepare for impending famine. It was during this famine that Joseph was re-united with his brothers, who didn't recognize him at first. Instead of causing them to suffer for their sins, he forgave and rescued them. His past had great purpose. A nation was saved. Despite and because of the pain others brought on him, Joseph knew he was right where he needed to be, for such a time as this.

Genesis 37-45

As Moses stared at the burning bush, he knew such a miracle was not of man. God called his name, and Moses replied, "Here I am!" Yet when God told Moses he was to lead His people out of Egypt and into the Promised Land, Moses was sure there must have been some sort of mistake. "Who am I that a Pharaoh would listen to me?" Questions. Questions. Questions. And the Lord God explained, "It's not about who you are. It's about Who I Am." Still, despite all the promises of signs and wonders, Moses worried, "I'm slow of speech and slow of tongue, Lord. You've got the wrong guy. Please. Send someone else!" Instead of an escape from the assignment, God gave Moses a partner and walked with him in His power. God made no mistake in His selection. A nation was saved. Despite his shortcomings, Moses was right where he needed to be, for such a time as this.

Genesis 3-4

Esther was made queen because of her beauty. Yet there must have been more to her charm. A woman who "obtained favor in the eyes of all who looked at her" is more than just a pretty face. As she sat in a place of power, her people were threatened by an envious officer of the king. Her heritage was a secret. No one had to know, as the Jews were destroyed, that the queen was one of God's people as well. But her godfather Mordecai encouraged her to do the right thing. Though she might be put to death for walking into the king's presence without his request, her position as queen was no accident in God's plan—she must do what she could to protect her people. And she did. A nation was saved. Because of her loveliness, Esther was right where she needed to be, for such a time as this.

Esther 2-8

If ever we feel our past sin is too big for us to tell others about Christ, we should immediately remember Paul. Once called Saul, a man who killed Christians, Paul's conversion proves that God's mercy is mightier than our misdeeds. Many were saved because of Paul's preachings then. Many are saved because of His writings now. Despite his past, Paul was right where he needed to be, for such a time as this.

Study

I once opened a piece of chocolate whose wrapper told me, "You are right where you need to be." I cried. Who cries while eating chocolate? Well, I did—because these words seemed so poorly timed. I was stepping through a period of intense suffering brought on by the lies and greed of others.

Years later I thought again of this chocolate wisdom—

which sounds an awful lot like Esther 4:14—as God placed me, deliberately I felt, in a job that beat me down daily. "Okay, God. I believe you. I do. But, really? I'm supposed to be HERE? Just tell me WHY!"

I've learned that sometimes the blessing that comes from "such a time as this" isn't ours to enjoy. Sometimes we get to be an instrument, through our pain, to reach and help others.

Also, not all "such a time as this" occasions are pleasant. Remember Joseph: sold into slavery, made high in the household of Potiphar, then imprisoned when Potiphar's wife lied about him. We like to focus on the moments of glory—the part of the story where he was second in command and saving Egypt. But maybe right now you aren't living in the peak—you could be in the prison. The way we act in the prison is what guides us to glory.

However, at other times we do experience the brighter and more beautiful perks of our life positions. We gain strength, character, and hope (Romans 5:3-5); we connect to God and His glory (Romans 8:18); we find peace in His presence (Isaiah 43:2); and we hold to the truth that we cannot be completely overcome, for God has already overcome this world (John 16:33).

These reassurances can help us in our journey to contentment in the now, the here, the "for such a time as this." God can use our present, even if it feels humdrum or disgraceful to us. God can use us where we are today. But we have to be willing to say "here I am" when He calls.

We can't stay in the pit other people throw us into; we have to climb out and see where His wisdom and strength can take us.

We shouldn't question how He can use someone as flawed or afraid as we are. We need to let Him be awesome when we feel inferior.

We cannot hide in the safety of unused gifts or opportunities. Sure, not putting ourselves out there means less opportunity for failure, but it also means we will lose who we really are. We need to take more chances to glorify Him.

We have no right to wait for someone "more qualified" and "less sinful" to speak on His behalf. We're all messed up; we all need Him.

He's here. He's always here. And He can use us here. Whatever is before us. Whatever He's calling us to do here—He's present, He's powerful, and He doesn't proffer what He cannot produce. We are here, to work with Him, for such a time as this.

1) What excuses do we use for not sharing God's influence and impact in our lives with others?

2) Which of these Bible figures do you connect most strongly with at this time: Moses, Joseph, Esther, or Paul?

3) What "time" do you feel you are in now: a term of transition, a season of waiting, a challenging duration, a time of blessing or reward, a stage of sowing, a period of preparing, or perhaps a mix of these?

4) How can God use you right where you are, for such a time as this?

Scrawl

Write out my adapted version of Esther 4:14 below.

You cannot remain silent and still. You are here for such a time as this.

Reread

Joseph

For such a time as this, I am here. No
harm intended will conquer the greatness
God can grant in this moment. And although
hate favors hate, love can overcome. Blessed
beyond and even through my past, I can
accept my present presence. I am here—
wholly where I am supposed to be, stand-
ing unholy before the Holy, clear-
ly quieted, warily aware of
my own flailing failings as I fathom
that forgiving others in His lush love—
no matter the depth of their deeds—becomes
an opportunity to take part in
the miracle of Grace defeating sin.

Sketch

Feeling inspired? Create something of your own:

- Journal about your own life and when you felt God placed you right where you needed to be "for such a time as this."
- Write your own poem about Esther, Moses, Joseph, or Paul.
- Draw an image that comes to mind as you read the sonnet or the stories of these Bible characters.

Devotional #2

"Live in the Wonder of God"

Start

In 1826, University of Oxford graduate and award-winning poet Reginald Heber wrote the lyrics to one of my favorite hymns. "Holy, holy, holy! Lord God Almighty! Early in the morning, our song shall rise to thee." Looking through the rest of the lyrics (below), we might be quick to judge the abundant usage of exclamation points (ten total in a four verse song). However, as an English professor, I'd have to say Heber didn't come close to going overboard. This particular punctuation is reserved for strong feelings and amazement, and I hope these are our exact emotions for the "blessed Trinity."

See

Holy, Holy, Holy! Lord God Almighty!
Early in the morning our song shall rise to Thee.
Holy, Holy, Holy! Merciful and mighty!
God in three persons, blessed Trinity!

Holy, Holy, Holy! All the saints adore Thee,
casting down their golden crowns around the glassy sea;
cherubim and seraphim falling down before Thee,
which wert and art and evermore shalt be.

Holy, Holy, Holy! though the darkness hide Thee,
though the eye made blind by sin Thy glory may not
see,
only Thou art holy; there is none beside Thee,
perfect in pow'r, in love, and purity.

Holy, Holy, Holy! Lord God Almighty!
All Thy works shall praise Thy name in earth and sky
and sea.
Holy, Holy, Holy! Merciful and mighty!
God in three persons, blessed Trinity.

Study

"Live in the Wonder of God" (which carries two excla-
mation points, a high volume for my personal style) is
inspired by Heber's hymn, Isaiah 6:3, and Psalm 8:3-4.
All three of these make me think about God's mighti-
ness, mindfulness, and magnificence.

Bible verses about God's awesomeness abound. Below
I've paraphrased a few more:

- If you ask the animals, they will give you an
  answer. The birds in the sky above us, the earth
  below, the fish in the ocean—all will tell you.
  They know who made them. Who doesn't know
  that God created all these things by His hand?
  Every living thing is the work of His hands, even
  the very breath of man. (Job 12:7-10).
- The sky proclaims God's glory—the heavens
  above show the work of His hands (Psalm 19:1).

- His invisible qualities are actually visible in His creation. This has always been true, and the obviousness of this truth leaves man no excuse to ignore Him (Romans 1:20).

The Bible tells us God is both everywhere and eminent. However, we tend to forget these facts.

Unlike much of my other work, this sonnet is more a series of pensive queries; it defies the typical Shakespearean style of presenting a problem and then answering said problem with the final couplets. Instead, my poem ends in yet another question.

This break from the classic setup is intentional. Most of us don't like unanswered questions. Leaving the reader hanging, so to speak, is my way of pressing us towards a time of true self reflection. My hope is that, as you read, you question your own tendency towards complacency.

Why are we so charmed by complacency? Is it simpler than living a life reflective of His greatness? Yet there is something in us that is empty without Him. Though it takes effort, we can embrace beauty over blah, awesome over eh, and wonderful over whatever. Let's make a veneration revolution. Let's proclaim His holy name. And let's trade in our complacency for intensity.

1) What elements of nature speak most to you about His awesomeness?

2) What tends to keep you from connecting with God's creation?

3) How can you find a way to connect with God's glory this week?

4) Find another Bible verse about God's greatness made obvious in His creation, and write it here.

Scrawl

Look back over the lyrics of "Holy, Holy, Holy," and write your favorite line below.

Reread

Live in the Wonder of God

"Holy, holy, holy is the Lord Al-
mighty: all earth is full of His glory!"
Call me then into your presence—enthrall
me with the awesomeness of your story.
Why does dullness pervade my days? Surround-
ed by the evercasting light of the
Everlasting Might of my God—dumbfound-
ed awe should prevail: not complacency.
But blindness to beauty becomes simple.
Too simple. Why? When the Maker of those
marvelous stars (all those stars!), is mindful
of me—in my frozen phase, I'm still chos-
en—why can't I live in the wonder of
God, when all earth is a sign of His love?
Isaiah 6:3

Sketch

Feeling inspired? Create something of your own:

- Compose another stanza to the hymn.
- Write your own poem about God's awesomeness.
- Draw an image that comes to mind as you read the sonnet or hymn.

the MAKER of THOSE marvelous STARS! is MINDFUL of me!

"Balaam"

Start

Balaam: most of us associate him as the guy in the
Old Testament who struck his donkey. I remembered
that and only that from this Bible story as I reread it
in a Wednesday night study on the book of Numbers.
That evening, I learned not only how much of the sto-
ry I'd missed in my childhood, but also how closely it
links to our lives today.

See

As Moses was leading the Israelites towards the land
of Canaan, King Balak of the Moabites sent word to
the sorcerer Balaam, hiring him to curse these Jews.
Because of his fear of God's people, King Balak prom-
ised a hefty financial reward in exchange for Balaam's
magic.

That night, God spoke to Balaam, warning him not
to meet with Balak and take the deal. Balaam obeyed.
King Balak sent servants back with a second request.
This time God told Balaam to go back with the ser-
vants, but to speak only the words He supplied.

On the trip to King Balak, Balaam's donkey began
acting quite peculiar. The animal perceived what the
men could not: an angel of the Lord was blocking the

path. When the donkey wouldn't proceed, Balaam beat it.

They continued on until, once again, the donkey saw the angel as the group trekked between two rock walls. To avoid the danger, the animal pressed Balaam and itself into the wall, injuring Balaam's foot. Again, Balaam hit the donkey, and they continued on.

A third time the donkey saw the angel, and this time it lay down, refusing to move forward. Balaam grew furious, shouting at the animal that then spoke in its own defense, "I've been your donkey for a long time. Have I ever acted this way? Doesn't my behavior tell you something?"

God opened Balaam's eyes, and he was able to see the angel for himself. "Why have you beaten your donkey? He was saving you from me. I've come because you are taking a reckless path against the Lord. If the donkey hadn't kept you from running into me, I would have killed you," the angel explained.

Balaam spoke, "I've sinned. I had no idea you were standing there. If God doesn't want me to go to King Balak, I'll just turn around."

"You still need to go with these men," the angel explained before repeating the words God told Balaam earlier, "but make sure you speak only the words God gives you."

After Balaam's arrival, King Balak once again offered vast riches for Balaam to curse the people of Israel, but Balaam obeyed the Lord. He declined the profits and blessed the people instead. This happened thrice; each time the king was hopeful Balaam would be tempted by the money, and each time Balaam explained he couldn't go against the command of the Lord at any cost. Eventually they parted ways. King Balak's intents were defeated. Balaam learned to follow the Lord completely.

If you want the full story, read Numbers 22-24.

Study

God is calling us to live with obedient hearts. Are we ready to listen and follow His lead?   If we are truly to walk His path, we must do so completely—heart, soul, and mind—without veering in some way we think will be a later advantage.

At first glance, Balaam seems to be obeying the Lord. But a man who doesn't see an angel right in front of him must have some ill intention in his heart. Balaam even holds a conversation with his donkey without being clued in that God is involved. It isn't until God Himself opens Balaam's eyes that he sees the danger he avoided. Then he's able truly to obey, even though he loses the chance at worldly prosperity.

Balaam's cautionary tale makes me think of several key scriptures.

- "For where your treasure is, there your heart is also" (Matthew 6:21).
- "What does it profit a man to gain the whole world but lose his soul?" (Mark 8:36).
- "Love the Lord your God with all your heart, all your soul, and all your mind" (Luke 10:27).
- "If you love me, keep my commands" (John 14:15).
- "Create in me a pure heart, and renew a steadfast spirit in me" (Psalm 51:10).

Finding one verse per Gospel (and one in the Psalms) was simple, because the Word makes clear that God wants our full devotion and attention. We cannot serve two masters (Matthew 6:24): God and our own desires.

I want to encourage us all to think about how often we try to sneak our interest into His intent. Sometimes we slightly alter His plans just enough to create what we think will be a better outcome for us. Maybe Balaam thought he could speak in such a way that he wouldn't technically be cursing Israel, but Balak could be convinced enough to pay the promised treasure trove. But God didn't want a slight obedience. He wanted full obedience. He wanted Balak to understand he couldn't step in between God and His people. He wanted Balaam to understand that following God's way is risky and may mean loss, but the real reward is far better than anything the world can offer.

1) What about this story stands out to you?

2) How can we make certain our treasure and heart remain with Him?

3) Why might we want to ignore roadblocks God is placing in our path?

4) Is God asking you, today, to walk a certain path with Him?

Scrawl

Here is Numbers 24:13, paraphrased. Copy it or write it in your own words below.

Even if someone offers me a palace full of gold and silver, I cannot go against the command of the Lord— for good or for evil—to make my own will happen instead. I will speak only His words.

Reread

Balaam

I see you standing in the way against
me, in truth for my own benefit—so
I may speak only of and from you. Since
the intent of my actions, I now know,
dictates whether or not I'm honoring
your orders with an obedient heart,
why do I still feel like maneuvering,
manipulating, modifying part
of your plan to better suit my schemes, to
alter your aims for my gains? How many
times does it take—even after I view
unmistakable signs of your plenty-
proof—for me to move forward in firm faith,
fulfilling your functions in me each day?

Numbers 22-24

Sketch

Feeling inspired? Create something of your own:

- Compose a prayer asking God for His will to lead your life.
- Write your own poem about your own struggles with the intent of your heart.
- Draw an image that comes to mind as you read the sonnet.

MAY I HONOR HIS ORDERS ➡» WITH AN OBEDIENT HEART

Index

In Times of Sorrow

In Times of Uncertainty

In Times of Change

In Times of Personal Reflection on Your Faith

In Times of Celebration

In Times of Discontent

When You Hear His Call

When You Feel Useless Because of Past Sin

When You Want to Reflect on Bible Characters

When Considering God's Grace

When You Need Motivation

When You Feel Like You Aren't Good Enough

When You Need Encouragement

When You Want to Remember His Greatness

When Experiencing Nature

When Pondering Your Purpose

When Struggling with Relationships

When Worrying about Perfection

When You Need to be Reminded of His Presence

When You Need to be Put in Your Place

When You Feel Anxious or Overwhelmed

When You Need to be Reminded of His Love

About the Author

Author Jessa R. Sexton is a write-at-home mom, former professor, sonnetierre, and crafting enthusiast. She has nine published books and has co-written two as well.

- *Saturday*
- *Rose-Pie*
- *Eldy and Ohi*
- *With Your Fresh Thoughts*
- *MoBert's Irish Experience*
- *Live the Blessing*
- *These Things I Pray for You: My Child*

- *Stories of Enchantment:*
  Twelve Fairy Tale Sonnets
- *Little Stories of Enchantment:*
  Twelve Fairy Tale Sonnets for Children
- *Educational Wellness*
  (co-written with Dr. K. Mark Hilliard)
- *Proverbs through the Generations (co-written*
  with Jack Hilliard and Dr. K. Mark Hilliard)

Jessa and her husband Jay love spending time with and talking about their children (Jack, Jonas, and June—yes, they all have "J" names, which was an accident at first and unavoidable after that), traveling, eating at new restaurants, and watching comedies. When Jessa experiences a rare moment alone, she watches classic television, composes songs and sonnets, reads, or gets lost in planning and goal setting.

The sonnet on the next page was written about six years ago but seemed appropriate to share here.

The Glamorous Life of the Mother-Poet

Have you ever tried to write a sonnet
with a two-year-old and three-month-old there?
Your witty thoughts are always lacking wit;
Your rhymes are forced, your meter less than fair,
You juggle iambic pentameter.
No one would claim you're writing without heart,
even though publication has no prayer.
Back in college you thought you were quite smart;
nothing could ever keep you from your art.
But now you find your inspiration changed,
no longer watching sunsets for your start,
five quiet minutes might could be arranged?
Don't worry, friend, it has to get better...
after you wipe the food off your sweater.

Afterword: A Note on Sonnets

The most famous sonnetierre (as I like to call myself)
was William Shakespeare. You've probably heard of
him. I find his sonnet form the easiest to write.

All sonnets have fourteen lines, each line with ten
syllables.

This ten syllable line is said to have iambic pentame-
ter. (An iam means two syllables; pent means five; two
times five equals ten, so the meter is ten syllables!)
Part of my style is to write in such a way that the ten
syllables are there, but the reading flows more conver-
sationally and less like a galloping horse.

The three most popular sonnet form rhyme schemes
are listed on the next page:

Italian

a b b a   a b b a

The remaining 6 lines are called the sestet and can have either two or three rhyming sounds, arranged in a variety of ways:

c d c d c d
c d d c d c
c d e c d e
c d e c e d
c d c e d c
c d c d e e

Spenserian

a b a b b c b c c d c d e e

Shakespearean

a b a b c d c d e f e f g g

www.ingramcontent.com/pod-product-compliance
Lightning Source LLC
Chambersburg PA
CBHW060334050426
42449CB00011B/2756